Easy
of West

G000255847

By Damien Enright

A Merlin Press Publication

Published by Merlin Press

ISBN 1 902631 05 6

Designed by Sean O'Leary
Photos by Damien Enright
Layout & Illustrations by Matthew Enright

MERLIN PRESS
Courtmacsherry, Co. Cork
Tel/Fax: +353 023 46045

Contents

Five easy loop walks on the western margin of Europe, in West Dingle's lovely scenery and clean air. Average distance from Tralee 60km, from Killarney 90km.

Dedicated to:
My patient wife, children, friends and dog
who have made life's roads a pleasure
and lightened my steps on the way

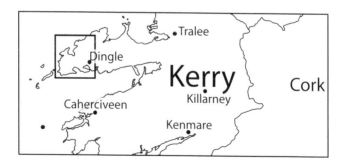

There is no guarantee that a walk outlined in this book is a right-of-way.
The author does not accept any responsibility for trespass nor for accident
or loss to or by the public in walking these routes.

INTRODUCTION

Kerry

West Kerry is a county with little climate, but much weather. The warm waters of the Gulf Stream wash between the open fingers of land. Mists or rain clouds drift in, like veils, off the Western Ocean. The sun, bright a few moments before, shines through them, like a spotlight sweeping the hills. Change is the only constant; take a short nap and when you wake you may think yourself in another country. 'Softness' is the theme, and water, a pellucid, magical light.

West Dingle

The people of West Dingle until recent times lived like the islanders offshore, and the small fields and bare stone walls we pass on these walks are not much different from those on the islands.

Here, at the cliffs of Slea Head, Europe ends. The homesteads and villages are last outposts; beyond them lies the Western Ocean. Traces of ancient settlements are everywhere, the stone oratories, the beehive huts, the ruined cottages and abandoned potato drills. The earth of West Dingle is sown with antiquity and, in lonely places, one can almost hear whispers from the past. Offshore stand the Blaskets, defiant but sea-worn, slowly saying good-bye to the land.

The Blaskets were home to a mere thirty souls when Robin Flower, an Englishman, visited in the 1920s. From that small population, he elicited three classic books, written in Irish, translated into English, Tomas ÓCrohan's *The Islandman*, young Maurice O'Sullivan's *Twenty Years a-Growing* and Peig Sayers' *An Old Woman Remembers*.

All are remarkable, but ÓCrohan's the most remarkable of all. His style and character were unique. His ironic description of the Blaskets as "*the last parish before America*" has become clichéd, but the poignancy with which he describes the death of his sons, and his beloved wife, will remain forever in the mind of a reader. His book is a testament to the faith and stoicism of a simple man and his neighbours. You would want to quote the whole book.

His eldest son went to get a young gull from the cliffs and fell. "*There was no wound or blemish anywhere on his body, though it was a steep fall from the cliff. We must endure it and be content! It was a great solace to me that he could be brought ashore and not left to the mercy of the sea.*"

Measles and whooping cough came to the island. *"Three months I spent sitting up with those of my children who took them worst, and I got nothing for the time I spent, only the two best of them were carried off. That was another discouragement for us, God help us. I fancy the sorrow of it never left the mother, and from that time she began to fail, for she was not to live long, and never lasted to be old."*

A few years later, a girl from Dublin got into trouble while swimming. Tomas's son threw down his spade, pulled off his boots and went to her help. *"He went, and he and the lady were drowned together."* The girl's parents came to Dunquin to the funeral... *"and had me pointed out to them. I hope they do not think I was angry with them because my son had died for their daughter. I was never so foolish as that. If it was for her he died, it could not be helped. It was God's will."*

But, if there is tragedy on the island, there is also great joy and humour, and a great spirit in the people. He speaks of selling lobsters to a passing vessel, a rare time of plenty *"It was a good life in those days. Shilling's came on shilling's heels..."* He tells of the bonanza of cut timber swept off the deck of a ship, of his childhood, his first visit to the mainland. He writes of matches and wedding feasts, of gathering seaweed, of seal hunting. He brings to life the love and faith of these unique folk

When we stand and look out of the Blaskets, his images leap and dance on the sunbright water. *"We are poor, simple people, living from hand to mouth. We were apt and willing to live, without repining, the life the Blessed Master made for us, often ploughing the sea with only our hope in God to bring us through. We had characters of our own, each different from the other, and all different from the landsmen. I have done my best to set down the character of the people about me so that some record of us might live after us, for the likes of us will never be again."*

The Blasket Islands were abandoned in 1953 and the islanders moved to the Dingle mainland, never to return.

for they dwelt upon a rock in the sea and not in a shining metropolis
and lived off the pick of the strand, the hunt of the hill,
the fish in the sea the wool off sheep, and packets full of dollars...
they were full of sunlight and mist, wind and stone, rain and rock,
but the Atlantic ocean would not pay them a regular salary...

extracts "Lucht an Oileain" by David S Quin

A note on walking.

The Irish are big on walking. If there is one thing we have plenty of, it is back roads and fresh air.

There are the power walkers, the Walking Women of Ireland, plugging along country roads with hips and shoulders swinging, out for the exercise after an already much-exercised day. The glow of their cheeks and the litheness of their stride attests the beneficial effects of 'exercise walking'.

Irish men, on the other hand, seem oblivious to walking's cosmetic effect, an unfortunate oversight on their part. Males are not seen striding along country lanes. When we do see a male abroad, he is generally being pulled along at a heart-stopping pace by two fist-fulls of dog leads, his greyhounds taking him for a run, rather than the other way around. Other encounters will involve men in caps, with fags in mouth and pockets full of fivers, out following the road bowling, after which they will walk miles.

There are the hill walkers and long-distance route marchers, doughty folk in serious boots, with ashplants, maps and small rucksacks. To them, we owe the opening up of green roads and byways, and the mapping of mountain trails not trodden since the ancient Celts made their way across country via uplands, the plains being covered with a dense growth of trees.

I, myself, do not power walk, greyhound follow, or road bowl wager. I walk for the curiosity and the uplift, the wonderments of the wayside and the 'high' of the free-flowing endorphins released after twenty minutes on the hoof. I am not so much a slow walker as one who is waylaid by the roadside attractions. Curiosity, atmosphere or amazement delays me, and while the company forges ahead, I am left behind, in thrall.

The walks outlined in this book are for walkers such as I. They take, generally, just a couple of hours but can easily be stretched to fill half a day. They are perfect for a weekend afternoon or a holiday meander.

They will, hopefully, stimulate my perambulating neighbours towards new horizons and inform visitors of the lovely land that awaits just off the tourist trail. I cannot imagine these local by-ways ever becoming crowded. We may in time meet a party of ardent Japanese, led by a person with a flag, or stout Austrians in lederhosen and braces singing *Falderee-Falderah*. They will be sure of a welcome. We Irish delight in showing off our land.

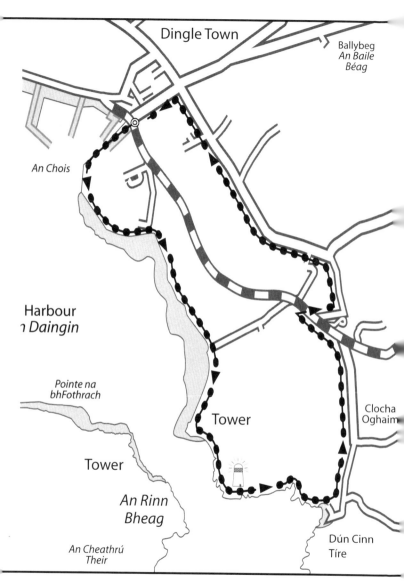

Dingle Town

Ballybeg
*An Baile
Béag*

An Chois

Harbour
n Daingin

*Pointe na
bhFothrach*

Clocha
Oghaim

Tower

Tower

*An Rinn
Bheag*

*An Cheathrú
Their*

Dún Cinn
Tíre

© **START**

1

Dingle Harbour Walk

From the town along the bay shore to Bhinn Bhán Strand at the harbour mouth, and back along the old Tralee-to-Dingle road.

Locality: OS Sheet 70 , Squares 4400, 4599 etc., starting at the eastern end of Dingle town.

Description and Distance: A loop walk, 7 km., 4.3 miles.

Walking Time: including viewing, 2 hrs.

Walking conditions: Pedestrian path, then field and cliff paths, and by-roads on the return.

Features: Only fifteen minutes from the town, we are in the world of nature, the coastline, the sea, the sea birds and the flora and fauna of the shore. We may see the Dingle dolphin close up as it follows the boats; the bay is narrow near the mouth. An interesting historic tower, and a quaint lighthouse. Then, a white-sand beach, with quiet back roads and wildflowers on the way home.

Flora and fauna: Ringed plover, greenshank, dunlin, turnstones; from September to May, there will be many waders, cormorants and ducks. In the summer, non-breeding oystercatchers in bright plumage will be seen along the bay, and stonechats and linnets in full breeding colours on the wayside hedges. Rabbits abound near Hussey's Tower.

Equipment: Ordinary walking shoes but in winter perhaps waterproof boots for the field paths.

Itinerary

(1) Passing the roundabout at the east end of Dingle town, we walk down the laneway opposite Moran's Garage. It is lined with small houses built in the 19th century by Lord Ventry to house fishermen he had evicted from An Rinn Bheag, a village across the harbour, having decided to make the whole Rinn peninsula a private hunting estate. Ironically — says Maurice Sheehy, writing in the late 1970s — the Irish Land Commission later bought the headland from Ventry and turned it over to local farmers; the fishermen remained in their cottages in Dingle.

(2) At the end of the lane, we reach the water. Looking right, we have a fine display of the Dingle fishing fleet, often in port at the weekend, and the pier. Some rust buckets lie decaying in the shallows. It is a colourful scene.

Dingle Town is as safe a harbour as one could hope to find, being almost landlocked and well protected by the hilly peninsula to the south west, the direction from which the prevailing winds blow. In the 16th century, it conducted a great trade with Spain, with Spanish galleons anchored in the harbour and many Spaniards living in the town. In the late 18th century, Marie Antoinette, having been taken captive by the Communards during the French Revolution, was offered sanctuary here by one James Louis Rice, a native of Dingle and a Count of the Holy Roman Empire. A house was made ready for her arrival, but she refused to leave France.

Kerry was the land of the MacCarthys, the O'Sullivans, the O'Donoghues and other Gaelic septs until, in the 13th century, it was partly overrun by the first wave of Normans. These, the Fitzgeralds, later to become the Earls of Desmond, intermarried with the Irish ascendancy, became more Irish than the Irish and, in time, fought against the English crown. They installed the Ferriters, fellow Normans, in West Dingle. Piaras Feirtéar, the last leader of that clan, continued to fight the English in the years after the final defeat of the Irish at Kinsale. He was the last chieftain to capitulate to Cromwell, under a safe conduct; this was dishonoured and he was hanged in Killarney in 1653. The wars of the 17th century saw the end of the power of the great Gaelic families. Kerry became defined as a county and Dingle as a borough, returning members to the British parliament. Landowners like the Fitzgerald Knights of Kerry and Lord Ventry dominated the political and commercial life of the town.

(3) We go left, on the made path along the shore. At low tide, there is a narrow beach and one can walk along the sand. At high season, the Fungi-viewing boats pass close by and we can hear the whoops and gasps of the besotted dolphin-watchers; indeed, we can sometimes see the good Fungi delight them with his tricks.

As we turn a corner, we see Hussey's Tower, also called Hussey's Folly, ahead. Ringed plover, pretty little birds with a black collar over a white breast and a black face-mask, run about the shore. Little ringed plover, a rarity from mainland Europe, may sometimes be found: the bill is all black, and there is a white line between the black mask and the brown crown. Often, the broken shells of quite large dog cockles are seen on the path; these will have been taken from the sand at low tide and broken open by ravens, grey crows or black-back gulls. Grey crows often drop them from a height to fracture them. In October, white, ink-cap mushrooms stand like candles in the grass, good to eat when the gills are pink but not after a night on the town; they are the source of Antiabuse, used in alcohol rejection-therapy. Do not eat after a wedding, a wake or a 21st!

We reach a stile; one has to be very slim to pass through and some walkers may have to briefly take to the shoreline. We cross a small stream. Often, here in the fields, in Autumn, one will encounter large flocks of small brown birds, up to 200 in number. These are young linnets, with a mix of other finches. Goldfinches and even bramblings are sometimes found amongst them. They forage in these big parties in winter, covering miles of land.

Amongst what may have been discarded builder's rubble is a stand of Japanese Knotweed, with red stems, and frothy white flowers in September. Japweed is a plague. It knocks over walls and grows straight through tar macadam. It subsumes and strangles all native plants. It was first introduced to Europe by one Herr Doktor von Siebold and, in 1847, won him a gold medal at Utrecht for the most interesting new ornamental plant. His garden had been home to over one thousand exotic species: soon, it was home to only one. Generations of gardeners have attacked knotweed with noxious substances, hoes and flame-throwers, all to little avail. Today, it thrives robustly on waste ground, roadsides, railway sidings and river banks. There is far too much of it in Kerry. Irish authorities will hopefully address the problem. The Knotweed Alliance, a UK group, are cautiously considering importing a fungus or insect parasite from Japan.

(4) We are now at the tower, or folly. The latter name seems unkind, because it was built not as a rich man's whim but as a charitable man's attempt to help the less fortune, the victims of the Potato Famine of 1847. Some sources say it functioned as a 'game lookout' and it was, apparently used as a watchtower by Excise men in later years. However, it was originally built for no other purpose than Famine Relief. Hussey was a tenant of Lord Ventry, and saw the construction of the tower as a way to provide the Irish with employment through which they could earn bread. There was no shortage of food in Ireland during the famine, only of potatoes, the staple diet of the tenantry; grain, vegetables and other produce continued to be exported to Britain and America. Trevelyan, of the British Treasury, decreed that these surpluses should not be made available free to the starving Irish. The maintenance of 'market forces' was paramount, a refrain we hear only too often in food emergencies today.

The tower doors and windows are blocked up, and cannot be entered. The brick work around the windows is attractive. It is noticeable that the wall on the seaward side is colonised by yellow xanthoria and similar lichens, while the other walls are almost bare. The vistas from this small promontory are excellent: Brandon, Mount Eagle, Stradbally, all are in view. Across the harbour, a shard of rock stands in the sea below the headland of An Rinn Bheag; black and dramatic, it is exciting when heavy seas break between it and the shore. The slopes opposite are wooded. This is the narrowest point of the harbour, and the Fungi boats are so close in that we can sometimes get as good a view of Dingle's famous dolphin as the folk aboard, who paid.

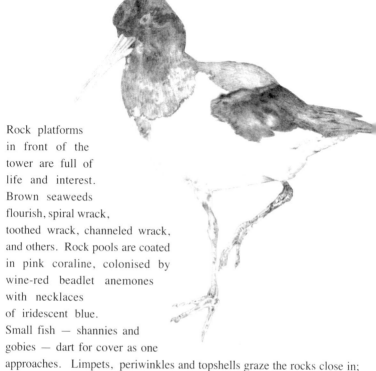

Rock platforms
in front of the
tower are full of
life and interest.
Brown seaweeds
flourish, spiral wrack,
toothed wrack, channeled wrack,
and others. Rock pools are coated
in pink coraline, colonised by
wine-red beadlet anemones
with necklaces
of iridescent blue.
Small fish — shannies and
gobies — dart for cover as one
approaches. Limpets, periwinkles and topshells graze the rocks close in;
further out, the shore is grey with acorn barnacles, millions of them.
Oystercatchers are common here, beautiful in their black and white
plumage, with vivid orange beaks and legs. Turnstones, smaller but also
black and white, forage amongst the weed which they turn over as they go.
Here, the birds are very tame and can be enjoyed at close range — unless
a redshank, the avian alarmist, spots one and, rising with a shriek like it's
been goosed, disturbs all others.

Burdock grows on the rough pasture just beyond the tower; its big leaves
have led to it being called 'wild rhubarb'. The hooked burrs which surround
the flowers attach themselves like Velcro to man and beast, a strategy to
carry the seeds to new ground.

From these rock platforms, a short distance along, 'Nancy Brown's Parlour', a famous cave can be reached. It is said to have been prepared for the landing of Marie Antoinette (see above) and to run all the way to the Presbytery House in Dingle, the residence of the good James Louis Rice, her would-be rescuer. The plan was that she would be landed here, at the harbour mouth, thus evading the natural curiosity of the Kerry people.

Two small strands adjoin, lovely places for children to explore the rock pools and bathe in the sheltered coves. A cutting through the low 'cliff' behind leads up to the fields; obviously carts came down here for generations, perhaps to fetch seaweed; deep runnels are worn into the bedrock by their wheels. Sea pinks brighten the low cliffs in spring and summer, and golden trefoil is draped like a cloak on their shoulders in June. The cutting takes us to the path along the field edge above us. Alternatively, we may reach it by climbing to the tower field and, via a purpose-built style beside a gate, continuing (along it) to continue between low hedges.

(5) On the promontory ahead, is the lighthouse, its neat keeper's house painted red and white, with a small boat slip in front. The light was erected in 1885. On the headland, opposite, is a watch tower, and a white-painted cairn of rock set into the cliff, a warning for shipping. Above, and further back, the dramatic Eask Tower is sited on a cliff nearly 200 metres over the sea, an arm of wood protruding from its dry-stone structure pointing the way into Dingle which, as a 'blind harbour', is difficult to find from the sea.

A worn path along the cliff side affords us wide views of the open ocean, with the gannets diving on the mackerel in summer, and terns passing in noisy parties — the young calling for food — from July on. Walking on the slippery grass below the path risks a fatal slide into the sea, and should be avoided. A mile further on, we come down onto the pretty strand of Beenbane, Bhinn Bhán in Irish, meaning 'white peak'. The sand is white, as the name promises. On summer days, the sea washes in gently and it is a fine place for a dip but, in the winter sou'westerlies, breakers crash and roar. There is a lifebelt on its post at the top of the strand. From the car park above, a boat slip runs down to the beach.

(6) Continuing on our way, we pass the car park, leaving the coast behind and making for the old road back to Dingle. For those who want a longer route, the coastal path continues past the beach, to Ceann na Binne, Beenbane Head, and a longer round, via Dún Séanna village, can be made.

The by-road is narrow and tarred, with a couple of old farmhouses and a few trees, these windblown. We ignore two right turns, and continue due north. Fuchsia, as usual, thrives on the roadside. We see the racecourse, in to our right, and Ballintaggart House, a period dwelling, now a Youth Hostel, ahead. Hart's Tongue fern is abundant along the roadside, often in deep shade. It is not a 'lacy' fern — like the tall male ferns and lady ferns and bracken — but has strap-like, waxy leaves, long and narrow, that shine like lacquer when they catch the light.

(7) At the main road, we turn left, and, after 150 yards, right, taking the sign for Pax Guesthouse, perhaps a Latin version of 'Suaimhneas' — meaning 'Peace' — a name popular with Irish B&Bs. Frilly lady ferns are now abundant on the roadside, and polypody ferns, toothed, with yellow spores clustered on the backs of the leaves. Honeysuckle - aka Wild Woodbine - also thrives on the ditches. Ivy is in flower from October onwards, often buzzing with harmless hoverflies and green-bottles that glitter like small jewels when the sun shines. The road goes sharply left, with a few 'sceacs' (blackthorns), just beyond, hardy survivors of whatever the Irish weather can throw at them, and sometimes bearing bitter, black sloes.

The road is gravelly, rather than tarred, just wide enough for a car. As usual, there is montbretia along the verge and we pass a good example of a traditional farmhouse, with very nice slate-roofed outhouses and a red barn slightly — as the antique dealers say — 'distressed'. A road joins us from the right; this is the old road into Dingle. Also to the right, in a field, is an impressive double-ring fort, almost 30 metres in diameter, with the ground within raised higher than the land around. Passing the Pax Guesthouse, we descend towards the town with its streets of tightly-packed, brightly-coloured houses; it has been said that the Irish are fearless with paint. A gate in the ditch affords us a panoramic view stretching from the harbour mouth west to Mount Eagle, with the town and its port in between, and trawlers moored along the pier. The stone wall on the right is old, and covered in lichen; it has, no doubt, seen many a weary traveller pass.

We come out on Sráid Eoin (John's Street), with multicoloured houses on both sides, no two painted the same colour. We reach An Droichead Beag (The Small Bridge), and turn left onto The Mall, with the old Courthouse and the Christian Brothers School, its beautiful garden climbing to a tall gable with a fine, arched window. We pass a large, white tableau of the crucifixion, and reach the roundabout, where we turn left. We soon arrive back at the garage where we began.

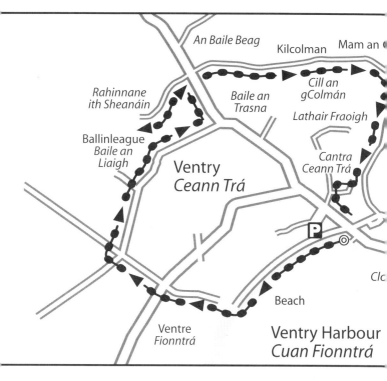

◎ **START**

The legendary Ventry Strand and St Colman's Grave

Taking in short sections of the Dingle Way and The Pilgrims' Route. Ventry village and Ventry Strand. Dunes and bog roads. Rahinnane Castle. Monastic site and ogham stone. Megalithic grave.

Locality: OS Sheet 70 , Squares 3800, 3700, 3701 etc.

Description and Distance: A loop walk, 7 km., 4.3 mls.

Walking Time: including viewing, 2.5 hrs.

Walking conditions: Beach, and back roads, with short stretch of field path.

Features: This is a walk full of variety, with the seashore and the hills, legendary sites and medieval history and pre-history. We begin at sea level and ascend to elevated views of Ventry Harbour and the distant mountains of the Iveragh Peninsula. The quiet lanes are edged with wild flowers. In good weather, we see the Skellig Rocks almost due south, thirty miles away but seemingly very close.

Flora and fauna: The dunes along the strand teem with insect and plant life in summer and will fascinate children and amateur botanists for hours.   Ringed plover and sanderling forage along the surf and, in winter, one may see red throated and great northern divers fishing offshore. Rabbits are seen on summer evenings, hares on early mornings in spring.

Equipment: Stout shoes are adequate for this walk.

Itinerary.

(1) We begin at the Post Office in Ventry, and walk across the R559 to a narrow lane leading down to the sea. We descend some steps and Ventry Strand, legendary scene of the longest battle and mightiest victory of the Fianna, lies before us, to our right. To the left is the Cliff of the Women, with a small promontory fort and traces of a house within. Here, the legend says, the womenfolk of the Fianna warriors resided during the years of conflict. Crede, who nursed the wounded and, after the last great battle found her husband, Cael, drowned on the shore, might have lived here. Cael, a Fianna warrior-bard, had won her heart by composing a poem in praise of her house as he passed through north Kerry. She followed him to Ventry Strand.

We reach the beach via a concrete walkway; some boulders may have to be scrambled over when the sea is full. Before contemplating the legends, it is well to walk some distance beyond the caravans at the start of the dunes. A caravan park is hardly appropriate in this setting but a view of the sea isn't only for the rich, and the site has provided economic family holidays over generations. Nothing marks this lonely shore as a place of legend, but the beach is vast when the tide is out, and wild in storms.

The legend has it that Fionn Mac Cumhail (Finn McCool), leader of the Fianna — a band of heroic huntsmen, warriors and poets who, in billowing cloaks and flowing hair, roamed Ireland in the 3rd century — ventured into France. There, in a scandalous *ménage-à-trois*, he absconded with both the wife and daughter of the French king. *The Encyclopaedia of Ireland* (Gill and Macmillan 2003) tells us that "Fionn's ability to attract women is well attested in the Fionn Cycle" (an 8th century epic).

The discomfited king sought help from his neighbour, the king of Spain, and from the mighty King of the World-except-Ireland. Their combined forces sailed into Ventry Harbour, bent on seizing the philandering Fionn and his *ménage*. The Fianna were hard put, over a year and a day of battles, to contain them. The foreigners had a champion — this was the age of one-to-one contests and battles in the Otherworld — who killed all warriors the Fianna fielded against him at the rate of one a day. A band of Ulster youths bravely marched south to confront him but each was killed in turn until the son of the Ulster king, in dying, dragged the giant underwater and drowned him on Ventry Strand. In a last great battle, Fionn killed the King of the World and won victory. Afterwards, the widowed Crede sat beside her husband's body on the shore and died of heartbreak, having composed a lament recalling how the birds and beasts, too, grieve their dead.

The irony for Mac Cumhail was that, preoccupied with retaining his French mistresses, he lost his only true love, the lovely Gráinne, who was four decades his junior. In the magic realism of the Celtic myth-world, Diarmuid Ua Duibhne, a handsome young warrior, watching the battle from a mountain top across the peninsula at Smerwick, saw Fionn engaged in other business and seized his opportunity to steal Gráinne's heart away. Together, they fled Ventry. Fionn, abandoning his interest in the French women, dedicated the rest of his life to their pursuit, but was unsuccessful. The name 'Leaba Diarmuid' (Diarmuid's Bed), found the length and breadth of Ireland, marks the far-flung places where the fugitive lovers slept.

The marram grass behind the beach holds fast the dunes.
Here, in August, we find burnet moths, their
black wings bearing six
vermilion blotches.
They feed on trefoil.
Later, their parchment-like
cocoons, fat with chrysalises, are
seen glued to grass stems, or
empty when the imagoes have
flown. Sometimes, the
yellow ragwort, attractive
but noxious — fatal to horses
if it is inadvertently cut and
dried in hay — is covered
in the black-and-amber

caterpillars of the cinnabar moth, a day-flying species which always seems torpid, especially after rain. Colourful banded snails roam the dunes, and common garden snails, the shells of which go white in this environment; perhaps it is the salt in the air. The flowers, often small, are pretty, like the dune pansies, delicate yellow and mauve, and purple sea bindweed which, unlike other bindweeds, does not climb over other plants but crawls along the sand. From July until April, ringed plover run back and forth along the surf; sometimes, also, sanderlings, and, in winter, dunlin, rushing about like clockwork mice. The tiny dunlin breed in Iceland; on migration, they have been recorded flying four and a half miles high. Of non-seabirds, the grey crow (aka hooded crow or scál crow, and not found in England or Wales) frequents the beach, scavenging on the tide wrack or tumbling spectacularly. Delicate, blue-and-white pied wagtails search the washed-up kelp for sandhoppers.

The wide but sheltered waters of Ventry Harbour teem with mackerel shoals in late summer, riffling the waters like fairy winds. Christy Moore, the folk singer, used the harbour as a setting for his amusing ballad about the famous 6th century Kerry saint, Brendan the Navigator, who, arriving back in Ventry after discovering America, announces his intentions...

> *"Everythin' was goin' great 'til Brendan did announce*
> *His reason for returnin' was to try and set up house.*
> *The girls were flabbergasted at auld St. Brendan's neck*
> *To seek a wife so late in life and him a total wreck!"*

In summer, the harbour is the venue of a famous regatta, with currach racing a major event. Currachs — long slim rowing boats, their light ribs originally covered in animal skins, now in black, tarred canvas — are called 'naomhógs' (nave-ouges) hereabouts, being the craft-of-choice for the wanderings saints (the 'naomhs') in centuries past. Brendan's transatlantic craft may well have been similar, but much larger (see Ballydavid Cliff Walk).

(2) We leave the beach via a wide cutting into the dunes about three quarters way along, where cars park. To our right, there is rough grazing, semi-salt marsh with flag iris, reeds and clumps of brambles on the tips of which the attractive little stonechats perch and sing. The male has a black head, white collar and russet breast; the female is also pretty, but less showy. Stonechats are typical birds of these wild places and are always seen in pairs. Yellow hammers, increasing rare, may also be seen.

The sandy path becomes a narrow lane, a fuchsia corridor leading up to the church. Opposite the church is Paidi Ó Sé's pub offering "Beoir agus Portar". A legendary Kerry footballer, four of his nephews who also played great football for Kerry live close by. Across the road is a stone house with a plaque commemorating the brief tenure, in 1892, of Jeremiah Curtin, a folklorist born of an Irish family in Detroit, USA. He collected the stories of the old people; although recorded in English, these folk tales are valuable because of their early date.

We now set off up the long, straight road towards the mountains — the rounded bulk of Mount Eagle to the left, and the pyramid shape of Cruach Mhárthain straight ahead. There are impressive cabbage palms (Cordyline Australis) in the garden of the house where the folklorist stayed. Native to Asia and Pacific islands, these trees are a feature of Kerry and West Cork, thriving in the mild Gulf Stream climate. In August, the roadside is bright with orange montbretia flowers, especially vivid when tossed in a strong wind on a bright day.

(3) We reach a four-cross-roads and turn right along a bog road, with stands of reed mace (bulrush), purple sedge and spiked reed in the wet fields on either side. Straight, narrow roads are typical of bogland. This one is the width of a single car, a lovely road to walk, with little, if any, traffic. Royal ferns grow on the ditches; these can be huge, sometimes creating a hummock of root stock that raises them a meter above the surrounding wetland. Foxgloves, sometimes two metres tall, line the route as early as May, as late as July. Of trees and shrubs, there is some low goat-willow, with silvery catkins in early spring, and the roadside fuchsia is especially brilliant in the yellow sun of autumn days. On the lower slopes of the hill on our left, we see small fields divided by heavy hedges and, higher up, just bare stone walls, the beauty of which can be the better appreciated with binoculars. Above them is the grey mountain, showing rock in places. Ironically, a state-of-the-art mast of satellite dishes is reached by a path between two old stone walls.

At a kink in the road, a farmhouse and a modern bungalow enjoy spectacular views across Ventry Harbour to the huge, blue hills of the Iveragh Peninsula — the Ring of Kerry — beyond. The bungalow has a Standing Stone, or perhaps a cow-scratching stone, in the front garden. Whether it is original or JCB erected, I didn't ask. Certainly, there is a Dingle fashion for having a Standing Stone, Stone Circle or Wedge Tomb in the front garden, a more robust variety of garden furniture than the gnomes of Surrey lawns. However, like the gnomes, megaliths amongst the shrubbery may not be as authentic as they appear. We now walk down an unbroken fuchsia lane perhaps half a kilometre long; the buzz of bees and drone flies fills the air on warm autumn afternoons.

(4) At the junction, there is a cluster of holiday cottages opposite, and we turn left onto a larger road, gently ascending, with a white line down the middle. After a few minutes, we come to an impressive stone on the left, inscribed "Árd an Caisleáin". A sign pointing left directs us to a guest house of the same name and Rahinnane Castle. Although our route goes right, down the minor road opposite, the short diversion to see the castle ruins, across the fields, is worthwhile. On the laneway, we pass a modern house with a steeply pitched, thatched roof and come to the large Árd an Caisleáin guest house where a sign invites one to enquire about access to the castle site.

Seen from the lane, the ruin is stark, grey and roofless against the fields rising behind it, in which sheep graze. The eastern wall is entirely collapsed, with the interior structure visible. Within the site itself, we appreciate the castle's true dimensions, built, as it was, on a more ancient double-walled ringfort. One of the largest and most notable in Kerry, this fort was clearly the seat of an important chieftain. The inside wall, sometimes as high as six metres, is still largely extant. In the 15th century, a fortified tower house was built on the site by the Fitzgeralds, and remained their stronghold until it was occupied by an Elizabethan force in 1602. Subsequently, it was returned to the Irish, but was destroyed by Cromwellian forces some fifty years later. The ruins may have been occupied for some time afterwards but were then left to the elements until partially shored up by the Office of Public Works in the late 1970s.

(5) We return to the main road and cross it to take the lane opposite marked by a wooden Pilgrims' Route/Way of the Saints fingerpost with the yellow symbol of the Celtic Cross and the outline of a pilgrim. Grass grows down the middle of this quiet bohreen. As we walk, we have wonderful views of the sea and the big Iveragh mountains — Knocknadobar, Mullaghmarakill and the Been Hills — and the high cliffs at the end of the peninsula, albeit with the Ventry caravan park in the middle distance. The views are breathtaking, and especially dramatic in the western, evening light.

Thrown out on the horizon beyond Iveragh's tip are the two Skellings. Small Skelling is the nest site of tens of thousands of sea birds, including 25,000 gannet pairs. Skellig Michael was, for many centuries, the remote redoubt of saints and scholars, a tower topped by two peaks, rising sheer out of the sea. All along the road, there is montbretia, brilliant orange in August, with tall New Zealand flax along a garden frontage to the left. The mountain pastures are grazed by sheep, the lower fields by cattle. A roadside Pilgrims' Route post indicates a field below us on the right in which the outline of the large monastic settlement of Kilcolman (Cill na gColmán) is still clearly visible although now reduced to low walls of stone. Here, is the grave of Saint Colman, its principal feature a stone carved with two Coptic crosses and an ogham inscription running over the dorsal saying "Pray for Colmán the Pilgrim". Only the foundations of the chapel remain. It is likely that pilgrims rested here en route to the summit of Mount Brandon, following The Way of the Saints, Cosán na Naomh.

We walk through a small hamlet and pass a well-designed, stone faced house with a tall, monastic-looking window, possibly inspired by the location. Between the houses, on the left, a rising path diverges to continue the Pilgrims' Route–Dingle Way, crossing the peninsula. We continue on the road, now going downhill. The Skelligs are straight ahead, nine miles out from the distant Iveragh coast in the sea so

wonderfully called the Western Ocean by ÓCrohan in his classic work *The Islandman*. This road is marvellous to walk at sunset, with the huge expanse of sky.

(6) We pass a sign carved in stone — 'Mám an Óraigh' the place of the springs — and then a quarry. Inside the quarry gate, on the left, there is a track uphill via which, the old guide books say, one can reach 'The Grave of the Munsterman' on the ridge above, but permission now should be sought to cross the private land. The grave, also called 'The Giant's Bed', is a megalithic tomb with the capstone still in place but the supports somewhat collapsed. There are many such artefacts in Munster and, with access difficult, it is hardly worth the effort but for the wonderful view.

Now in sight of the caravan park and the beach, we find a Pilgrims' Route fingerpost, with an arrow pointing to the right, down a narrow track with fuchsia on both sides. Taking this, we pass through the ruins of a farmhouse and yard and then reach a small road. We turn left and soon come down onto a larger road. About one hundred yards further on is the Post Office and pub, where we began.

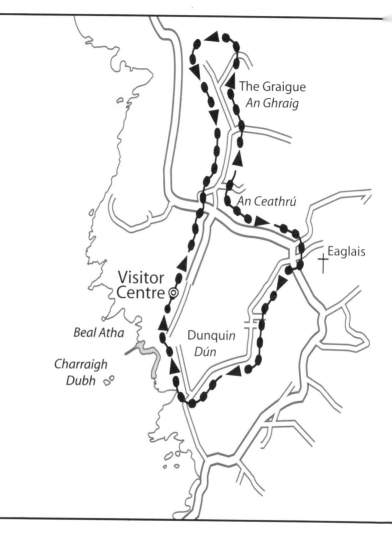

The Graigue
An Ghraig

An Ceathrú

Eaglais

Visitor
Centre

Beal Atha

Dunquin
Dún

*Charraigh
Dubh*

◎ *START*

21

The Blasket Visitor Centre Walk

After the Visitor Centre and its story of island life, a walk out of doors takes us into the very air and weather of the islands. The wind, when there is wind, blows in off the shoulders of the Great Blasket, and the small fields and bare stone walls along our route are not much different from those across the Sound. The unique spirit of place, of the western edge of Europe, here pervades the land.

Locality: OS Sheet 70 , Squares 3200, 3201 etc.

Description and Distance: Walk A: A loop walk, about 4km, 2.5 miles, mostly on road but including a grassy path by a stream leading to a lonely cove facing the islands. One section requires a short scramble; otherwise, a very easy walk.   Walk B: Also a loop, incorporating Walk A but with an added round on off-road tracks with panoramic island views. Distance, 6km, 3.7 miles.

Walking Time: Walk A: approx. 60 minutes, Walk B, approx. 90 minutes.

Walking conditions: Back roads, unpaved tracks

Features: Quiet backroads, pretty streams, with many wildflowers in spring and summer. Marvellous views of Inishtooskert and over the dorsal ridge of the Great Blasket.

Flora and fauna: Gunnera, winter heliotrope, montbretia, fuchsia, japweed — all the 'garden escape' plants that have naturalised waste ground and stream banks in West Kerry's mild climate. An odds-on chance of seeing the bird that walks underwater, the Dipper.

Equipment: Comfortable walking shoes.

Itinerary:

(1) We leave the Visitor centre and turn left, along the tarred road. Black knapweed — or "hardheads" — is in unusual abundance along the ditches, with a bright purple flower blooming from June to September. It is becoming less common as old meadows disappear under silage-grass prairies. With its disappearance, country girls may find it harder to get a preview of their marriage prospects. In the past, they only had to drop a knotweed head, with unopened buds, down their bodices and consult them a half an hour later. If the buds had opened, they were sure to marry soon.

This short stretch of road is full of arcane romance. On the ditches, there is also some Dwarf Western gorse, the low, wiry kind, our only variety before the Normans brought the taller French gorse to the UK and, later, to Ireland. An old country adage says: "Kissing is out of season when gorse is out of bloom." Country people know that there isn't a day of the year when there isn't a sprig of yellow gorse blooming somewhere. Thus, as bodice-expanded knapweed brings hope to repining maidens, so may blooming gorse give unkissed bachelors cause for hope.

23

(2) A few minutes up the road, a grassy path between hedges runs off to the right at 90 degrees – I'll call it the Gunnera Path. It can be clearly seen, crossing between fields to some houses on a higher, parallel road. If it is passable, it can provide a very short and interesting loop (2.5km, 1.5mls) back to the Visitor Centre. However, half way along, it dips and the hollow isn't well drained; it may be passable only in rubber boots. It seems unlikely anybody would object to walkers using it; it goes through boggy farmland, with sheep. A drainage ditch, in the wet spot, wouldn't be hard to dig. I imagine that, in times past, a wiry Dingle farmer could have dug a runnel in a single morning, armed with a narrow-bladed spade. It would surely be worth while for the County Council or the Visitor Centre to make efforts to open it; it would add an invaluable amenity to a visitor's enjoyment, at low cost.

An interesting feature is the stand of gunnera beside the roadside stream one crosses to enter this path. Gunnera, like an exotic rhubarb — or elephants' ears, when it dies back and becomes grey — is a massive plant, under which one could almost conceal a car. Like fuchsia, it comes from South America and thrives in the mild, Gulf Stream climate of Ireland's west coast, now colonising bogs and stream courses — even cliffs in Achill Island, in Mayo. Fixing nitrogen from the air, there is a danger that it may overwhelm native bog plants, adapted to low nitrogen soils.

(3) If the Gunnera Path is open, one may shorten the walk by half a mile; however, the sure option is to continue on the tarred road to Ceathrú cross-roads. Here, we may take Walk 1 or Walk 2.

"Ceathrú" is carved into a granite boulder by the roadside, with an adjacent post crowded with brown signs indicating local heritage venues. An Oige Youth Hostel is on the corner. Here, Walk A turns sharp right, following the tarred road and leads us, via a loop down to the sea, back to the Visitor Centre. To take this route, turn to paragraph (6) below.

(4) To follow Walk B, we go straight ahead, on the narrow road ascending between houses and finger-posted for The Kerry Way. Brilliant blue field scabious brightens the verge and, then, surprisingly, a small patch of purple-flowered, five-petalled meadow cranesbill, a plant shown in the authoritative Blamey and Fitters *Wild Flowers of Britain and Ireland* as occurring only in Donegal, Antrim and possibly on the fissured limestone pavements of the Burren. Passing a nice, low stone house on the right, the sudden, raucous quacking of ducks may make one jump; they would be at least as good sentries as the geese that saved Rome. On the rocky Kerry peninsulas, stone houses are more harmonious in the landscape than white ones; indeed, the green and lovely plains of Western Dingle are not improved by the widespread scatterings of white-painted houses. In the past, they would have been grey, and not intrusive on the drama and beauty of the land.

There are marvellous high fuchsia hedges along here, sonorous with the sound of bees on warm September days. We pass stone houses with tar-paper roofs, in the tradition of the Blaskets.

(5) The tarmac ends and we continue on the wide, unpaved track ahead, marked The Kerry Way. It shortly splits; we take the right fork. From here, we have a spectacular view of the Blaskets Beginish, to our right, big from this perspective although Beag Inish means "Small Island". The massive bulk of Great Blasket is to our left, below us, so that we can see the full length of its high dorsal ridge. Between these two, further out, Inishtooskert, "Northern Island", a pyramid of rock, rises out of the sea. The intrepid St Brendan had a lonely oratory on the western side, facing the vast ocean; perhaps from there he contemplated his voyage to the west. Low black rocks, like teeth, are scattered between the mainland and the big islands, the waves breaking over them; some have a few green acres, and once provided grazing. The Skelling Rocks are twin pinnacles rising from the empty ocean far to the south.

When the sun shines on the Great Blasket, the White Strand is golden across a blue sea. It looks benign and inviting, the great, green island rising in a hump behind the beach. A few minutes later, the scene may be dark and forbidding, as cloud passes over. When the mist is down, the islands are ghostly mountains, frozen in the grey sea.

One thinks of Tomás ÓCrohan's book, *The Islandman*, and his stoic acceptance of a life where sons and fathers were drowned in sudden storms, and the shawled women waited on cliff tops with no hope but prayer. One thinks of the fathers and sons themselves in the open boats, with no power but their arms on the oars to keep them from the toothed rocks and dangerous shore.

The track we follow was made for the filming of *Ryan's Daughter*, an event still remembered — and benignly exploited — here in Dingle. The film introduced Dingle to the world as a place of breathtaking beauty and its 'locations' are still a draw. This is the road to the 'British Camp', and the remains of the film village is only a short diversion from here.

In the Spring of 1968, the stars, ROBERT Mitchum, SARAH Miles, et al, walked these paths. I have found peonies in bloom there, surely not AN indigenous species — perhaps they WERE the progeny of seeds from a film star's overblown bouquet.   A raven croaks overhead, a true-born native. The track across this moor looks as if it might go on forever; ahead, there is not a house or an artefact in sight. At the highest point, we enjoy a wonderful view to Smerwick Harbour and the village of Ballydavid across two stretches of water, with the magnificent Three Sisters and Sybil Head sweeping skywards to our left.   Sybil Head was called for Sybil Lynch, a rebellious daughter of the Lynches, one of the Tribes of Galway.   She eloped with a Ferriter of Dingle in the 15th century and, chased by her father, hid in a cave on the headland, where she was drowned by the tide.

A path now bears left towards an impressive rock pile, the oldest boulders in Dingle, standing stark against the sky.   Spewed from a volcano some 400 million years ago, it is called The Graigue, An Ghráig; for the hardy, it is worth climbing for the roof-of-the-world view it affords.   Our path passes close beneath it and, just beyond, we enjoy a panorama of the west side of the Great Blasket not seen from Slea Head or Dunquin; and Inishtooskert is very prominent, now. Through the binoculars, the neat stone-walled fields on the Blasket are visible, but Beginish has no fields and seems entirely inhospitable. Stonechats are ubiquitous in this wild country; they perch on the thistle tops, even if they are swaying in a gale. The beautiful wheatear can often be seen here in summer, the white flash of its rump and the black inverted "T" on its tail as it bobs amongst the rocks, dwarf gorse and bell heather make it unmistakable.

This is a prime place from which to watch the sun set behind the Blaskets, a wonderful photo opportunity on a clear evening or when the sun, like a giant beam through the clouds, focuses on the islands or diffuses in a grey haze over the sea. No mainland habitation is visible, only the houses on the Blasket, deep in green shadow. Time stops; even the sea seems without motion or sound.

The track has taken us around in a figure-of-nine, and we head back down to the tarred road again, past the barracking ducks. We turn left at the Ceathrú cross-roads and rejoin the route of Walk A.

(6) We walk along the tarred road east from the Youth Hostel. The land to the north-east rises to the pyramid of Cruach Mhártain mountain. We shortly take a secondary road to the right; almost immediately, we may stop to admire the famous "Kruger's" pub, legendary watering hole of Hollywood stars, travellers, troubadours and talkers seeking the romance of these last redoubts of Europe.

Kruger Kavanagh was a Kerryman who went to America and worked in show business: in his portrait, on the outside wall, he looks like a tough Bowery priest. In the 1920s, he came home with a pocket-full of dollars and bought the bar. So many friends had he made in his profession that, until his death in 1971, American stars of stage and screen regularly came to visit him. Indeed the choice of Dunquin for *Ryan's Daughter* — and, later, Hollywood's *Far and Away* — probably arose indirectly from movie-lands familiarity with the stunning scenery as seen from the back window of Kruger's pub. Distinguished only by the Irish-language plaque commemorating Kruger as "Irishman, walker and storyteller, 1894 -1971", the front of the establishment is refreshingly unassuming for such a legendary place. His nickname arose from his favouring of the Boers over the British in South Africa, a sentiment widely shared in Kerry at the time.

We shortly pass a house on the right which carries a plaque to the writer, Séan O Catháin, "a noble Blasketman". Seen between the modern bungalows on the road side, Inishtooskert is prominent again, with a clear view of the peak of rock that, from some prospects, seems like a church spire rising behind the backbone of the Great Blasket. Beyond the O Catháin house, where a by-road goes off to the left, a typical old farmhouse survives, with three dormer windows.

A great furrow runs down the rump of Mount Eagle to the south carved by a stream. Across the sea, the houses on the Great Blasket seem close, because they are white. In the past, a few were lime-washed but even these blended modestly into the grey-green land, barely-noticed human footprints on the great island; now, they seem large and detract from its grandeur. One hopes An Bord Pleanála and Kerry county planners will not allow inappropriate development. As an icon of our heritage, surely the physical and spiritual proportions of the Great Blasket should be preserved.

The road descends steeply. Some walls have been cleared to make fields unusually large for these regions. We cross a small bridge, a pretty spot, the stream babbling between banks of montbretia, a South African garden 'escape' that harmlessly lights up the countryside in late summer.

Here, also, is the lovely fuchsia, Deora Dé (God's Tears) as it is called locally, an alien from Chile that does no harm. Sinister, however, is the white-flowering, red-stemmed Japanese knotweed that crowds the right bank below the bridge. This alien colonises above ground, by seed, and below ground, by rhizome. It has, so far, proved impossible to eradicate in the British and Irish Isles. Uncontrolled, it threatens to subsume the landscape, drowning its fellow aliens, the fuchsia and montbretia, and all native growth.

We now see that the stream bank is swathed in japweed all along its course. We pass some nice houses on the left, and see the Blasket Centre over to our right; it is not as well landscaped as the Skellig Visitor Centre at Valencia on the Ring of Kerry, which is roofed with sods. Flocks of starlings, numbering hundreds, are often seen in the fields, hereabouts. This is a very pleasant road to walk. At a hand-painted sign, "Cul-de-Sac", we take a left, down to the sea. The Blaskets are a constant presence. From here, Inishtooskert looks like Skellig Michael — far to the south and not visible — a typical profile of an Atlantic sea-stack. The track is rough, but fine for walking. We pass two stone houses, sensitively restored, with Blasket-style tar-paper roofs.

(7) When the track ends, we are immediately on a green path with bell heather on our right as we come down over the stream. This is a beautiful section of our route and a lovely spot for a picnic. At a way-mark post, we turn left. The Blaskets are low on the sea. The stream is on our right, tumbling over small waterfalls to a pool below us; it splits around stony islands of montbretia, and rocks splashed white with lichens. Here, one often sees a dipper, like a large, black robin with a pure white breast, standing on rocks and bobbing its tail. The dipper has the uncanny knack of walking underwater — not swimming, like ducks or cormorants, but walking along the pebbled bottom of fast flowing streams, stalking caddis-larvae and crayfish and creatures that dwell amongst the stones. White flowers dot the watercress on the surface. Japweed grows here, too.

The stream flows to a small beach and joins the sea. Off shore, is a black rock, "Charrig Dubh". Bladder rack and kelp lie washed up on the small strand, where we ford the stream, the smell of iodine pungent in the air. At the far side, we ascend to a broken tarred track, then to the tarred road proper. Royal ferns are on the ditches and a bog is on the right, with flag iris flowering yellow in May and June. Tall flowers of the wayside verges are, in their season, foxglove, purple loosestrife, common figwort and meadowsweet. The stone walls nurture wall rue and hard ferns. After five minutes, we find ourselves back at the Blasket Visitor Centre where we began.

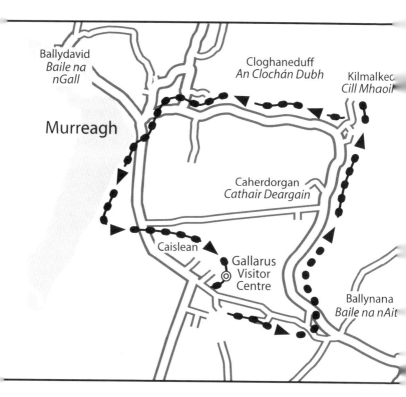

Ballydavid
Baile na nGall

Cloghaneduff
An Clochán Dubh

Kilmalkec
Cill Mhaoi

Murreagh

Caherdorgan
Cathair Deargain

Caislean

Gallarus
Visitor
Centre

Ballynana
Baile na nAit

◎ **START**

Gallarus and Kilmalkedar

A walk full of history, starting at Gallarus Oratory. Cathair Deargáin stone huts, once the home of an important chieftain, the Chancellor's House, Kilmalkedar Church and ancient centre of learning. St. Brendan's House. Many fine views.

Locality: OS Sheet 70 , Squares 3905, 3906 etc.

Description and Distance: A loop walk, 8 km., 5 mls.

Walking Time: including viewing, 2.5 hrs.

Walking conditions: Pedestrian paths and side roads, beach.

Features: From the fifth to the thirteenth century, West Dingle was the retreat of saints. The prayer houses and churches we visit are so simple and durable in their construction that one can only think the designers were inspired. At Kilmalkedar, a centre of learning during our 'Era of Saints and Scholars', we find, side by side, oghams stones with the old script and alphabet stones carved with the new Roman letters. All is set against the beauty of the land and the stone-walled fields sweeping down to Smerwick Harbour.

Flora and fauna: Murreagh strand has fine rock pools which, for child or adult, are well worth exploration, especially between the months of April and October. Many shoreline birds are present in winter and wheaters may be seen in summer.

Equipment: Ordinary walking shoes

Itinerary.

(1) As we set out from the Visitor Centre at Gallarus, the view behind us is of the Three Sisters, peaks of land sweeping dramtically upward from the plain to summits 700m above the sea. We take the neatly gravelled path — signposted Gallarus Oratory — towards that unique prayer-house created by a master craftsman thirteen centuries ago. Nothing was used but stones. The design is inspired; perhaps one of the saints designed it. It is now as it was then — or, at least, as it became a few summers later, when the new lichens and wall rue had begun to colonise its walls.

Simplicity and durability are the outstanding features of Gallarus Oratory. It is modest. It is functional: it is of the place: it is organic. It wears and weathers like the stones of the walls and the fields; it grows gardens of mosses; it shelters minute life. It is a testament not only to the durability of materials and design, but to the resilience of the faith that raised it. For thirteen hundred years it has stood. Not an alteration has been made, not a stone has been stolen. Time has colluded with the stones; only the wooden door that sealed the entrance has succumbed.

Clearly, the early saints understood the beauty of simplicity. The shape is that of an upturned boat, the sides curving gracefully up to the keel (which is the roof-ridge), all built in stone. Light pours through a single shafted window in the gable; its proportions make it a work of art.

Not only does this oratory still stand; it is bone dry inside. The dust underfoot is powdery. In winter, when storms sweep in over Smerwick and the Sisters, the air inside the cell hardly moves, a candle doesn't flicker, the buffeting of the wind cannot be heard. In daylight, motes of dust hang in the shaft of light from the window; the passage of the sun is tracked on the dust floor. This quality of beauty and durability was achieved in the 8th century, with no tools but a hammer and chisel for shaping stone.

One September, we saw a swallow feeding its young in a nest under the roof vault. Swallows know a good nest site when they find one, and return generation after generation. Perhaps, as the old saint prayed, they watched the bird's ancestors take first flight through the shaft of the window into the blue vault outside. The land rises behind, with stone walled fields, and houses scattered here and there on the lower levels. On typical Atlantic days, the sun pierces the clouds like a giant searchlight sweeping across these hills. Dark at one moment, they are dazzling green at the next. Ballydavid village basks in sunlight, and the blue sea dances beyond.

(2) We take the pedestrian path to the tarred road, where we turn left. It is a narrow road, a fuchsia corridor in places, climbing gently; if there is traffic one has to stand well in. Ahead, stone walls climb the flanks of the hills, following the contours. A disused roadway crosses the mountain almost horizontally. We pass an old farmhouse, with stone buildings, and the climb gets a little steeper. Other farmhouses we pass are being 'done up'; it will soon be hard to find an original farmhouse on the south west coast of Ireland, but hopefully bad chests and lumbago will be but a distant memory. We come upon a plaque of cut stone set into a wall telling us were are in the townland of Baile na n-Ath. Opposite, is an unmade short-cut to the main road, fifty yards ahead. We take this and cut off the corner. We then go left, on a main road. It can be busy in peak season but we will not be on it for long.

34

When visibility is good, the views to the left are stunning. In good weather, the sea is brilliant blue ahead. As the road descends, the ground rises steeply to the right, with great lumps of rocks in the fields. The views of Smerwick Harbour are magnificent, with the whole stretch of Wine Strand, near Dun an Óir. Perhaps the name comes from the *wine – from the Royal Pope* as James Clarence Mangan described the Papal force that landed there in 1580 to support the Catholic cause (see Ballydavid Cliff Walk).

(3) A long straight road — with the name Cathair Deargáin on a cut stone at the top — runs off to the left but we ignore this and continue to a stile, 150 yards further along, which gives us access to the Cathair Deargáin settlement, once probably the home of an important chieftain.

Overlooking a big sweep of land between it and the sea, it comprises an impressive, well-preserved collection of five hut foundations within a ringfort. The hut walls are more than a metre thick and over two metres high, curving inward. The roofs, once thatched or covered in sods, have succumbed to time. The chambers are interconnected, with fine stone lintels, very low, and evidence of, perhaps, souterrains, where food or valuables might have been stored beneath the floor. Their view is spectacular; this settlement had a commanding position over all the plain stretching as far as Murreagh Strand and what is now Ballydavid village. Across the harbour is Wine Strand, with Binn Diarmada rising against the sky beyond, and Cruach Mhárthain and Mount Eagle to the south.

Immediately in the view below is a house, well-landscaped, with a dark slate roof, ribbed like a Chinese parasol. Towards the sea to the left is a bungalow, painted pink at the time of writing, with a Standing Stone in the front garden. This stone seems to be the real thing rather than an example of Kerry JCB art. One can imagine archae-ologists in a thousand years time scratching their heads and trying to decide which standing stones are the real ones. The stones themselves will have equal antiquity irrespective of how long they have been standing, and if the house has long perished how will the experts tell JCB-transported garden ornaments from Neolithic menhirs? And, anyway, the fact that a stone happens to stand in a front garden doesn't mean it is 'wrong'.

(4) To the right, a few hundred yards beyond the Cathair Deargáin settlement, our route takes us past other stone ruins, Tigh an tSeansailéara, the Chancellor's house, the 13th century home of the Chancellor of Ardfert Diocese. Its impressive size indicates the status in which the nearby church settlement of Kilmalkedar was held.

(5) Kilmalkedar is an Anglicisation of Cill Maolchéadair and, like most Anglicisations, fails to reflect the Irish meaning, the 'Church of Maolchéadair'; Kilmalkedar gives us only the sound of the name. Maolchéadair was an Ulsterman who founded a monastic settlement here in the 6th century. Why he choose remote West Dingle, so far from his birth place, is not known. However, the most important ecclesiastical foundation on the peninsula grew up here, with a Romanesque church built in the 12th century, its corbeled stone roof a development of the style found at Gallarus Oratory. On a plaque outside, it is described as "a precise Irish Romanesque cathedral in miniature". The elegant chancel arch within is carved with chevrons and the gable houses a tall, narrow window, splaying inward, the "eye of the needle", through which the very slim of figure might manage to squeeze and, according to legend, achieve salvation.

There is evidence of an older wooden chapel on this site and the surviving church was also a school, a centre of learning in the era of Saints and Scholars, when Britain and mainland Europe were in the Dark Ages. Students of the well-to-do came to Ireland for education, while stalwart Irish monks journeyed forth to bring learning to the heathens. Within the church is a 'classroom aid' from the 7th century, an abcedarium stone with the Latin alphabet, newly introduced, carved in its face and a simple cross. This is probably the oldest surviving relic of Roman lettering in Ireland.

Also inside the church is a holed stone, evidencing much earlier pagan worship at this site, and there is a similar stone outside, with ogham markings reading MAEL INBIR MACI BROCAN, Mael Inbir, son of Brocán, the holed stone being a symbol of rebirth. Apparently, the early Irish scholars were not iconoclastic; they left the evidence of earlier beliefs to stand side by side with their own. The ogham script is still legible, faint and worn, no doubt by rain. One is reminded of Thomas Hardy's poem, *"Down their carved names the rain drop ploughs..."*

Close by is a crude stone cross, dramatic in simplicity and resilience, a symbol, perhaps, of robust Celtic Christianity, the faith before the Roman frills. Such crosses are rare; others stand at the remote monastic settlement on Skellig Michael, 700 ft above the sea. The graves to the right of the church are almost all of antiquity, some marked with mere stumps of stones, some large tombs overgrown with tussocks, and some with fine Celtic crosses, these more modern. The Kerry tribal names, O Súilleabhain, O Conchubhair are prominent, and some unusual local names: one Mott Grummell and his sister Nell Malone (Grummell) are remembered. By the church door, an inscription asks for the mercy of God on the people of Murphy of Bhaile Liosce, who lie beneath the stone. The view afforded the dead is quite magnificent, with the unfortunate inclusion of an electricity cable running across it.

(6) We leave the church grounds via a path through the more modern cemetery, with black marble headstones. Back on the lane, a sign indicates the Pilgrims' Route to the right, the old Way of the Saints to the summit of Mount Brandon, the path of the great pilgrimages to St. Brendan's shrine. In to the left, is the two storey St. Brendan's House, a priest's dwelling house of the 15th century. The house is entered by some steps; a plaque gives details of its history. Below it, neatly encircled by a stone wall, is the small St. Brendan's Well, with thriving wildlife, whirligig beetles on the surface, algae and orb spider webs on the walls, a perfect place for frogs to spawn. It is still traditional for the devout to visit the well and nearby graveyard on Easter Day. Many of the artefacts at Kilmalkedar are associated with cures — the ogham stone was apparently effective for epilepsy.

(7) Back on the road, we go right, descending gently, the sea ahead. A few hundred yards along, a narrow path to the right, fenced with a neat wall and sheep wire, takes us to a gravelled enclosure with an oratory somewhat smaller than the Gallarus. This, the Argail Bréannain, Brendan's Oratory, predates Gallarus; its modest structure almost fades unnoticed into the land. The roof is gone, the walls of undressed stone lean slightly inward.  Again beautifully designed and expertly constructed, a low doorway under a stone lintel gives access. Inside we find a stone altar, and a simple, splayed window at the rear. This is a quiet place, with few visitors. Behind it are the empty hills, with a sprinkling of sheep.

(8) Further along the road we pass houses with cordyline palms in the garden and luxuriant lichens on the roofs, testament to the mild, damp weather. We see the steeple of the Church of Ireland, built in 1860 and now deconsecrated, the congregation having dispersed or died off. During the Famine upheavals, the burgeoning Protestant population of Dingle attempted to expropriate ancient Kilmalkedar as its centre of worship but, frustrated by local Catholic opposition, built this church instead. For all its steeple and big windows, the churches and oratories built more than a thousand years before it seem to achieve a closeness to the simple Christian ideals which this — and many ornate churches — do not.

(8) The road now passes between houses — the village of An Mhuiríoch — and we can go straight ahead onto Murreagh Strand. The small stream to our right has sticklebacks under the banks and small eels, like bootlaces, under the stones, also small dabs, in summer. It is half choked with watercress but it is not advisable to eat watercress from any stream that passes through sheep land, part of the life cycle of the worm that gives sheep the dreaded 'staggers' being spent in watercress stems.

To the right are rock outcrops, with stands of kelp and oarweed, and rock pools teeming with life between early May and late October. All the usual shellfish — the various winkles, whelks, acorn barnacles and limpets — abound, and there are gorgeous sea anemones clinging to the sides. Of the small fish, shannies are in almost every pool and are a marvel of adaptation to an environment which can be precarious in big seas. Their front fins create a suction pad to glue them to the rocks, and also serve as 'feet' with which they can scramble from pool to pool as the tide recedes. Shannies have no scales, the better to allow them to squirm into crevices. They can live out of water for much longer than most fish, having a mucus on the skin which allows them to 'breathe' by a kind of osmosis; thus, they are found in sheltered estuaries in May, the breeding season, gathered under rocks when the tide has gone out and is not due to return for hours. Montague blennies are of the same family, with a small top-knot on the head. Both species are 'puppy dog' like, with hatchet-shaped heads and bodies narrowing to the tail. They are brown, green, or olive, depending on their surroundings; changing colour is another talent of the blenny clan. Pipe fish, relatives of the sea horse, scorpion fish (harmless) and gobies are also common.

The beach is host to many birds in winter. Oystercatchers, black and white with orange beaks and legs, can be found all year, but winter brings the migrant waders, dunlin, rushing about like wind-up toys, redshank, shrieking in alarm when one comes near, greenshank, very elegant and whitish-grey, turnstones, ringed plover and whimbrel.

We walk left along the beach — Dun an Óir and Cruach

39

Mhárthain are landmarks in the distance, dead ahead. The strand is very wide when the tide is out, a bracing beach when there is a breeze. Tellins, dog cockles and razor shells litter the sand which is often beautifully grooved by the tides and dotted with the small pyramidal casts of lugworms. We pass a line of boulders laid between the shore and water, and beds of pebbles, multi coloured and very pretty when wet. Some 600 yards further on, we reach a point where cars come down onto the sand. We turn left here; there is a distinct cutting in the dunes.

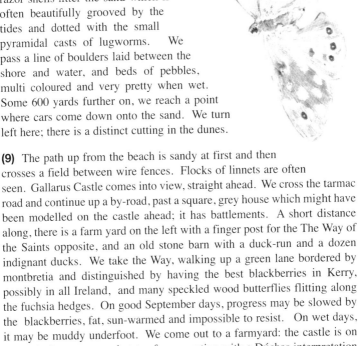

(9) The path up from the beach is sandy at first and then crosses a field between wire fences. Flocks of linnets are often seen. Gallarus Castle comes into view, straight ahead. We cross the tarmac road and continue up a by-road, past a square, grey house which might have been modelled on the castle ahead; it has battlements. A short distance along, there is a farm yard on the left with a finger post for the The Way of the Saints opposite, and an old stone barn with a duck-run and a dozen indignant ducks. We take the Way, walking up a green lane bordered by montbretia and distinguished by having the best blackberries in Kerry, possibly in all Ireland, and many speckled wood butterflies flitting along the fuchsia hedges. On good September days, progress may be slowed by the blackberries, fat, sun-warmed and impossible to resist. On wet days, it may be muddy underfoot. We come out to a farmyard: the castle is on our right, in a very good state of preservation with a Dúchas interpretation board and a kiosk where visitors must pay a fee to enter the castle in the summer season. Built in the 16th century, it was a Fitzgerald stronghold. The last of the family to live there was Patrick Fitzgerald who, on his death bed in 1688, asked to be taken to a window whence, looking out over Smerwick, Wine Strand and the Three Sisters, he remarked, "What a grand day for a Geraldine to die..."

The car park at Gallarus is only a few minutes down the path. There is a cafe which serves cakes and tea.

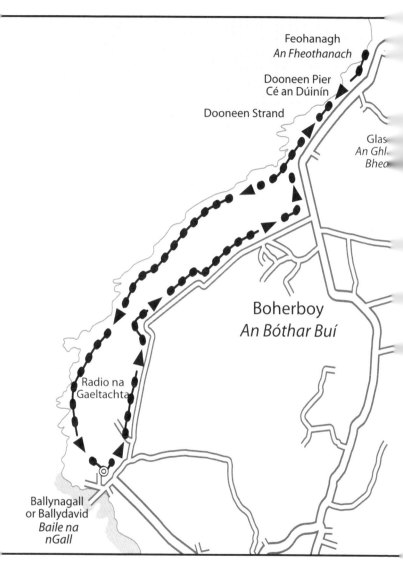

Feohanagh
An Fheothanach

Dooneen Pier
Cé an Dúinín

Dooneen Strand

Glas
*An Ghl.
Bheo*

Boherboy
An Bóthar Buí

Radio na
Gaeltachta

Ballynagall
or Ballydavid
*Baile na
nGall*

◎ **START**

41

Ballydavid Cliff Walk

Back roads and then, a cliff top path, part of the Dingle Way.

Locality: OS Sheet 70 , Squares 3807, 3908 etc.

Description and Distance: An easy loop walk of about 6 km, 3.5mls, especially scenic in the late afternoon or early evening.

Walking Time: less than 2hrs

Walking conditions: Back roads, off-road tracks.

Features: Currachs, and the pier from which St. Brendan is said to have sailed to America. Quiet backroads, pretty streams; many wildflowers in spring and summer. Dramatic views of Inishtooskert and the dorsal ridge of the Great Blasket.

Flora and fauna: Impressive rock pools, deep enough for snorkelling. Wild vegetables of the sea shore. Diverse lichens.

Equipment: Comfortable walking shoes.

An introduction.

Reading the Ordnance Survey map in English, one will see two Ballydavids. The Ballydavid of our route is Baile na nGall, on the north shore of Smerwick Harbour. The other Ballydavid is Baile Dháit, an inland village on Ballydavid Head. While the British map makers somehow overlooked the difference, the Irish people would have known that Baile na nGall was 'the town of the foreigners', referring to a Viking settlement in the 9th century (Smerwick means 'the butter harbour' in Norse) while Baile Dháit was, simply, 'Dháit's homestead'. English-speaking visitors are confused, even today.

The route is exciting at any time of the year. We are on the western edge of Europe; only the broad Atlantic lies between us and Newfoundland. In spring, when the wind is from the south, swallows coming in from Biscay make a landfall here, the last leg of their migration from the African veldt to Irish barns. Swallows are 'site faithful', and find their way back, over the deserts, mountains and seas, to where they were born. In summer, when the sprats are inshore and mackerel shoals riffle the surface like wandering breezes, gannet from the Skellig colony dive-bomb the ocean just below our path. Autumn brings whales, fin whales, pilot whales and minkes; with luck, one may see the white pillars of spume rise against the blue ocean as they blow. In winter, the sea itself is the thrill, the deep oceanic swells throwing themselves onto the land, the wind in one's ears and the spray flying.

We begin at Baile na nGall, built above the beach on Smerwick Harbour, its two white strands divided by a pier, with a pub conveniently located above each. The loop comprises a tarred road on the outward leg, going north, plain but full of interest, and a cliff path on the way back, walking south. There is the chance of seeing the sun set behind Dún an Óir (the Fort of Gold), the Blasket Islands and the Skellig Rocks, and the opportunity for a fireside drink in one of the pubs or, weather permitting, a sundowner outside.

Itinerary.

(1) Setting off, with the pier behind us, we keep left on the road, passing between houses. The road divides again; we keep to the left fork. A ridge of hills to the right rises to the eroded peak of Reenconnell, with rock showing through. Tall, creamy meadowsweet swathes the verges in August. Elizabeth the First thought it the best flower for masking the robust smells of the 17th century. It makes marvellous, sleepy wine.

We pass the tall, slim mast of Radio na Gaeltachta on the left. There is a small bungalow dwarfed alongside it, perhaps quarters for the programme presenters or those who take the graveyard shift.

The road is narrow and, therefore, a little difficult if there is a lot of traffic; however, heavy traffic is rare. There are various ditch flowers, often of great beauty, and varying with the months of the year. Celandine is abundant, the first flower of spring, like a child's drawing of the sun couched in a foliage of green, heart-shaped leaves. Celandine closes when clouds pass over, or when there is rain. Later in springtime, there are wild daffodils and yellow flag irises, the *fleur-de-lys* that is the French national symbol, in the boggy fields. Towards the end of the summer, flaming red montbretia is everywhere, while figwort, very tall and almost shrubby, is common, along with pink willowherb and purple loosestrife. Tormetil, a pretty, yellow, four-petalled flower, small and bright amongst its green foliage, blooms into October, with pink Herb Robert bringing a bit of colour even on winter days.

As we walk, we see Binn Diarmada, northern most of the Three Sisters headlands, sweeping gracefully skyward beyond the mouth of Smerwick Harbour. Sheep graze in the roadside fields. As the road briefly swings east towards the hills and Reenconnell, there is fuchsia on the left and montbretia on the right; this is an especially lovely stretch in August. In September, fleabane grows in patches near the pink cottage with sunflowers in the front garden and a radio mast in the back. Just beyond, in a front yard, is the surreal sight of four beer keg look-alikes mounted on short posts. Perhaps they have some connection with the mast; I have met no-one who knows.

Now, to the right, an unpaved road between a half-mortared farmhouse and an old outhouse leads to the hamlet of Bóthar Buí (Yellow Road) with some newly built houses and – like everywhere, now, in Ireland – others going up. There is new affluence and employment in remote places where, traditionally, more than half of the young people emigrated, most, never to return. The 'American wake' — the 'funeral'-cum-good-bye-party held for the beloved child going away — is now a thing of the past; even if they go, they return, and tourism, technology or bit parts on Radio na Gaeltachta or TnaG can help provide them with a living at home. Indeed, TnaG, the Irish language TV station, seems to have a cast of hundreds. The girls are all very modern and good looking, and can act while speaking Erse. Does acting talent come with fluent Irish? It seems every second person born in the Gaeltacht — if not a musician, dancer or writer — is a 'natural' for the camera or the stage.

(2) At a T-junction, with huge Mount Brandon straight ahead, we turn left. The land sweeps gently up towards the low cliffs, northward; a house we pass has a neat rick of black turf in the yard, like a miniature Gallarus oratory. The motif of the boat is never far away on the coast of Kerry; we have the old saints' oratories, like upturned boats, and the ricks of turf, and the black currachs. Even some of the mountains — the north ridge of Mount Eagle — are shaped like upturned boats.

We see the sea ahead now, as the road descends gently past Gorman's Clifftop restaurant. Binn Diarmada is to the left, Ballydavid Head to the right with a black rock (another Charraig Dhubh) offshore, white water breaking over it during storms. As we pass an unusual house with a semicircle of front windows facing the view, there are sea pinks on the seaward side of both ditches; they thrive in the salt air. A sign saying 'An Ghlaise Bheag' points to the village of that name, and we pass a roadside factory, producing Irish couture.

Now, we see Dooneen Strand ahead, with houses above it. On the right, a hydrangea hedge a hundred yards long leads across a field to a cottage. The road passes over a small watercourse full of montbretia, flowering in August; the name 'An Ghlaise Bheag' means 'End of the small stream'. It is worth while stopping to look down over the parapet. In late summer, the winding path of orange flowers, with the stone wall speckled in white lichens and the dark pool trapped between seaweed-covered rocks, makes a marvellous photograph.

Just beyond the 'bridge', one can cross a rough field to the left and find a way down to Dooneen Pier on a beaten track through the grass, but there is a twelve foot drop at the end that requires some climbing skills to negotiate. Better to walk along the road, and turn down opposite The Old Pier Restaurant.

(3) On the way down to the pier, we pass some naomhógs, their shiny black hulls turned skyward to protect the laths that form their rib cage from the rain. Called currachs in Connemara, their Kerry name translates as "the small boats of the saints" because they were the craft in which the saints wandered the islands of Ireland and Scotland — "naomh" means saint. For voyages far out into the western ocean, a heavier craft, with sails, would have been required.

The rock pools outside the pier are magnificent; at low water they can be waded and at mid tide can be explored with a snorkel and mask. The sea rages over them in winter, and deposits kelp and oarweed by the ton. The cliff walls are veritable gardens of vitamin C, where a sailor could harvest tangy, dark-green sea beet, succulent rock samphire and bitter scurvy grass to bolster his health on a long voyage.

From this pier, brave St. Brendan and his crew of muscular monks sailed west in the 6th century, their cowls around them, seeing God in the waves and the winds and the sea birds and sustained, no doubt, by chant and prayer. They alternately rowed and sailed their cowhide currach far west, through sea ice and icebergs, recording their journey in the *Navigatio Sancti Brendani*. In 1977 authenticity was lent to this account when Tim Severin, intrepid adventurer and seeker-after-knowledge, carefully reproduced the craft Brendan might have sailed in, launched it from Brandon Creek and proved possible what Kerry people always knew was true — that a Kerry man had navigated the coasts of the New World centuries before the Vikings, the Basques or Christopher Columbus set sail.

Perhaps, in the initial stages of their voyage, the saint and his monks ate sea beet and rock samphire gathered on the cliffs above the cove. They might well have fermented a brew of scurvy grass, as did herbalists twelve centuries later, to keep its Vitamin C effective after weeks at sea. Thus — far out in the ice floes in the fogs of the Grand Banks — merry song may have punctuated the prayer-chant, off the cliffs of Newfoundland.

After the pier, we retrace our steps to the road and turn right, back the way we came, to the black-and-yellow road sign indicating a left curve. Our cliff path begins behind it, a small sector of the beautiful Dingle Way.

(4) The path is well worn, gravel at first, then trodden earth. Fifty feet below are black rocks and the sea, with a rock pool big enough to swim in and, when the weather is wild, big swells rolling in. Here is a good place from which to watch the sun set behind the Three Sisters. In times of high Atlantic cloud, there will be sunbeams chasing one another across them. Sheep wool, wind-blown on the barbed wire, can make these cliffs feel bleak in winter, but the sea is at its most alive and dramatic when the land is dead.

We pass another tall mast broadcasting to places afar, and then some big stones with skeins of sea ivory sprouting from them, like a grey-green

Neptune's beard. As the name implies, this lichen is an indigent of the seashore. Other lichens also grow here, most prominent the brilliant orange xanthorias, like yolks of seagull eggs splattered on the rocks. When the mackerel are in, in summer, this is a great perch from which to watch the gannets. The terns are lovely too, as they plunge-dive for sprat, the young, hatched in Iceland only a month before, wheedling and harassing their parents for scraps. These tern families are going south, following the sun. Some will follow it almost to Antarctica, and then follow it north again. They stay with us awhile on each passage. God speed the terns!

There is a blasted heath as we near a communications mast, wild in windy weather. Ling heather finds cracks, and flowers from the bedrock, as does dwarf gorse. In spring, the yellow flowers of silverweed dot the salt-burnt grass and sea ivory flourishes on the low walls alongside the path, probably undisturbed for centuries. Modern technology ascends in its glory from a rocky field, a tall antenna held erect by a web of steel cables, anchored in concrete against the ferocity of the storms.

Now, on any reasonably clear day, Skellig Michael may be seen framed between the Great Blasket and the Iveragh mountains as if all were the same distance away. In fact, the Skellig is thirty miles south, and the Great Blasket only seven. Such are the illusions of the pearly light. In the foreground is Smerwick Harbour, Dun an Óir and all its adjacent strands.

Approaching two more masts, we cross a field of low heather, Wine Strand and the long white strands on the south shore of Smerwick Harbour now very visible across blue sea or grey. At an elbow of the path where there is sheep wire guarding the cliff edge, one might stop and watch the sea rise thirty feet at a heave and throw bubbles of spray aloft and make the surface look like churned porter. It would not be unusual to hear a party of choughs overhead and look up to find them tumbling and diving, red beaks, red legs, our glossy feathered crows, raucous spirits of the western edge of Europe. We are proud of our Irish choughs, plentiful here, sadly almost extinct in the UK.

The path is eroded in places and it is sensible to stay well in. We cross a small stream. In wild weather, bubbles of spray fly overhead like wraiths on the wind. There is ruined concrete watch-hut to the right of the path, a World War II relic. Across the waters of Smerwick Harbour, we see Dun an Óir, the Fort of Gold. Behind it, across the neck of land, Skelling Michael and The Great Blasket float far away on the southern sea; Dun an Óir has a history at least as notable as either. Built on an ancient promontory fort, it was, for generations, a stronghold of the Ferriters, an Anglo-Norman clan. In 1580, a Papal force of 600 soldiers, mainly Italians, with some Spanish and Irish, landed here to support the Irish Catholic cause — *wine -- –from the Royal Pope... And Spanish ale shall give you hope*, as James Clarence Mangan later described it in *My Dark Rosaleen*. The English bombarded them mercilessly from land and sea until they surrendered, 'with honour'. All in the fort were then slaughtered, men, women and children. Present during the siege and massacre were the gentle poet, Edmund Spenser, author of *The Faery Queen*, and Sir Walter Raleigh. Both received vast tracts of Munster for their services to the crown.

The route now descends gently. In wild weather, the big rollers riding in to Mhuiríoch Strand run parallel to us as we walk, and break on the black rocks below the path. We soon arrive back at Baile na nGall, where the hospitality of the hostelries awaits us.

Illustrations